SO-AQD-417

The
Man Who
Split Time

22 Proofs Jesus Is God

Phil Johnson
Todd Friel

GOSPEL
PARTNERS
MEDIA

Reaching the lost. Together.

The Man Who Split Time

Published by:
Gospel Partners Media
3070 Windward Plaza, Ste. F301
Alpharetta, GA 30005

© 2020 by Phil Johnson and Todd Friel. All rights reserved. No part of this publication may be reproduced, stored in a retrieval system, or transmitted by any means—electronic, mechanical, photographic (photocopying), recording, or otherwise—without prior permission in writing from the publisher.

Edited by Lynn Copeland

Page design and layout by Genesis Group

Printed in India

ISBN 978-1-7340532-2-7

What Kind of Mortal Can Split Time?

Imagine a man who lived such an extraordinary life that Western civilization changed the entire calendar system to commemorate his birthday. The obvious question would be, "Who was that man, and what did he do to deserve such an unprecedented honor?"

That man doesn't have to be imagined; that individual is Jesus Christ. Time is divided into BC (Before Christ) and AD (*anno Domini*, "in the year of our Lord") because of this one incomparable person.

For this reason alone, you and I are wise to carefully consider, "Who is Jesus Christ, and what did He do to split time?"

For centuries, Western civilization answered that question, "Jesus Christ is God manifest in the flesh who entered time to save sinners from the wrath of God." Only recently has there been an attempt to whitewash the impact of His life by changing BC and AD to CE (Common Era) and BCE (Before the Common Era). There is a reason for this squabble over letters.

If Jesus Christ is just a historical fabrication, then we are free to disregard everything He supposedly said and did. But if Jesus Christ is indeed God in the flesh, then everything He taught has massive implications for you and me.

- Jesus Christ claimed to have exclusive qualities of deity.

- Jesus Christ claimed rights to your personhood.

- Jesus Christ claimed to be the only way to everlasting life.

- Jesus Christ claimed that if you fail to acknowledge Him as your Lord and Savior, you will perish when you stand before Him on Judgment Day.

If you aren't currently agitated, I doubt you read that last bullet point. Considering the source, that was a downright scary threat. The Man who changed time claims that He is going to judge you and consign you to hell if you don't acknowledge Him as your God. What is that all about?

Why This Is Such a Big Deal

As you are going to read, Jesus Christ didn't just make His debut on the human stage two thousand years ago. Since the beginning of time, God the Father promised He was going to send God the Son (Jesus) to deal with our biggest problem: sin.

You and I do things our consciences warn us not to do (we lie, cheat, and steal; become prideful, angry, and jealous; have racist and sexist thoughts; watch porn; have sex outside of marriage; etc.). We are like guilty criminals who have broken earthly laws, only our situation is much more dire—we have broken God's eternal moral laws.

Because God is just and good, He must punish lawbreakers. But God is also rich in mercy, and He desires to offer a pardon to guilty lawbreakers. But here's the rub: if God simply dismisses our court case, then He would be unjust and unloving.

If one of your loved ones was viciously murdered, for instance, you wouldn't be too happy if a judge simply let the killer go free.

Just like a good earthly judge cannot release heinous criminals, God *must* see that all evil-doers are punished. And here's the bad news: our penalty for breaking the laws of a holy God is capital punishment—the death sentence.

But there's good news. God actually loves guilty criminals, and He provides a way where He can be just and, at the same time, justify the unjust. God the Father sent God the Son to be our Savior—to bear the punishment for the crimes you and I have committed. Talk about amazing grace!

Jesus came to earth as the promised Messiah, or Christ, to intentionally lay down His life and appease the wrath of God for those who have sinned against God. The King of the universe bore the death penalty for His rebellious servants. God died for the ungodly. The Creator gave His life for His fallen creation.

Guilty sinners who repent and trust in Jesus Christ as Lord will have His payment applied to their account. Forgiveness and mercy will be theirs, and everlasting life awaits them. On the other hand, wrath and eternal judgment await those who refuse to bend the knee to the Lord Jesus Christ. The stakes in this debate couldn't be higher.

If Jesus Christ is a mere mortal, then eat, drink, and be merry; your life is pointless, and you will spend eternity as worm food. But, if Jesus Christ is indeed God, then your life has meaning, and your eternity will be spent in heaven or hell.

Asking, "Who was Jesus Christ, and what did He do?" isn't mere academic folly; it is the most practical and important question you will ever ponder. Your life and eternal destiny depend on your answer. In other words, you have to get this right.

How Can We Know?

Let's take a look at the evidence and see where it leads. We can confidently do that because Christianity is not a blind faith, it is an *eye-witness* faith. The Bible is a reliable collection of historical documents written by eyewitnesses during the lifetime of other eyewitnesses.

This is crucial. When you read the historical accounts of Jesus Christ, you are reading *eyewitness* testimonies from men who lived with Jesus and were willing to die for what they saw with their own eyes.

Christianity Is Not a Blind Faith

Imagine ten men who declare Jesus is the Son of God are on trial for their "blasphemous" belief. These ten followers cling tenaciously to their testimony claiming to have seen Jesus do supernatural things. They are not blindly parroting stories they were told; they steadfastly refuse to recant because they *saw* Jesus do things that only God can do.

The court threatens them with a gruesome execution if they won't retract their claims. Nevertheless, they refuse to betray the truth. For their stubbornness, they are rewarded with torture, crucifixion, beheading, hanging, immolation, and a dip in a Jacuzzi filled with boiling oil.

If these men merely believed myths about Jesus, it is certain that most, if not all, would have denounced their belief that Jesus is God. But *none* of them were willing to do that, despite the gruesome consequences. These men didn't merely believe Jesus was divine, they *knew* He was God in the flesh because they had seen Him act and speak like only God can. The apostle John wrote:

> What was from the beginning, *what we have heard, what we have seen with our eyes, what we have looked at and touched* with our hands, concerning the Word of Life...*what we have seen and heard* we proclaim to you also. (1 John 1:1–3)

That is why Christianity is not a blind faith, it is an eyewitness faith. Prepare to read *reliable* eyewitness accounts of the things Jesus did and said that demonstrate beyond the shadow of a doubt that Jesus is God.

Here are twenty-two proofs that Jesus Christ is indeed God in flesh.

1 Jesus Does Miracles

Copperfield, Houdini, Angel, Blaine, Blackstone. These men are very clever magicians, but there is a reason the calendar was not re-

written because of them: they are mere illu-
sionists. All of their tricks can be explained as
optical illusions or mere sleight of hand.

On the other hand, Jesus Christ did count-
less miracles that can only be explained if
Jesus is God. You will not find a Las Vegas
magician who would even dare to attempt
what Jesus did.

- Jesus fed thousands of people a meal from
  only a few fish and a few loaves of bread
  —twice (Matthew 14:15–21; 15:32–38).

- Jesus raised people from the dead, including a man who had been in a grave for *four
  days* (Matthew 9:18–26; John 11:14– 45).

- Jesus changed a minimum of 120 gallons
  of water into wine without the aid of
  computer-generated smoke and mirrors
  (John 2:1–11).

It's one thing to do magic tricks; it's another thing to perform acts that defy the laws
of nature. Watching a Vegas magic show causes
an audience to say, "Oooh, aaah." Watching a
man make food miraculously multiply and

raise people from the dead should cause you to say, "That man is divine."

2 Jesus Heals Diseases

Sadly, these days you will see videos of Christian charlatans on the streets claiming to do a "miracle" by lengthening someone's leg. This is a silly parlor trick that demonstrates these hucksters are criminals, not divine healers. Jesus, on the other hand, healed so many people that He virtually wiped out illness in Israel. These are just a small sample:

- Jesus performed genuine organic healing miracles (Matthew 9:1–8; 12:10–13), including ten lepers at once (Luke 17:11–19).

- Jesus made blind people see (Matthew 9:27–31).

- Jesus made the deaf hear (Mark 7:31–37).

- Jesus made the lame walk (John 5:1–9).

Only God can instantaneously and completely heal organic illnesses. Not once did Jesus say, "Sorry, Bub, I can't heal *that* malady."

Jesus healed each and every sick person who came to Him because He is the warmhearted God who has the power to heal the sick and lame.

3 Jesus Has Authority Over Nature

Imagine you are in a boat when a sudden storm causes waves to crash into your little dinghy, which is quickly filling with water. A man rebukes the wind and it instantly obeys His command to be still, leaving the sea perfectly calm (Matthew 8:23–27). What would you conclude?

You would hardly think this man had played a parlor trick on you. No doubt you would conclude what the disciples concluded when they saw Jesus *walk on the sea* and calm a raging storm: Jesus is God (Matthew 14:22–34).

It has been rightly said there is not a molecule in the universe over which Jesus doesn't declare, "Mine." He orchestrates and orders the things that are seen, and He rules over everything that is unseen. Mere mortals can control very little; Jesus controls everything, including nature.

4 Jesus Is Omniscient

Soothsayers are quite predictable. For a fee, they will offer vague generalities that can hardly be considered reliable or supernatural. Even popular psychic Sylvia Browne admitted, "Only God is right all the time." Repeatedly Jesus demonstrated He knew people's specific thoughts (Matthew 9:3,4; 12:25; Luke 6:8; 9:47). He also demonstrated that He knew their precise activities (John 13:11).

When Jesus encountered a woman in Samaria, He told her that she had five former husbands and was now living with another guy. Recognizing that He was the Christ, she then testified to the townspeople, "He told me all the things that I have done" (John 4:39).

In another instance, a man named Nathanael was so persuaded of Christ's omniscience that he immediately began to follow Him.

Jesus saw Nathanael coming to Him, and said of him, "Behold, an Israelite indeed, in whom there is no deceit!" Nathanael said to Him, "How do You know me?" Jesus answered and said to him, "Before Philip called you, when you were under the fig tree, I saw you." Nathanael answered Him, "Rabbi, You are the Son of God; You are the King of Israel." (John 1:47–49)

Not only did Nathanael never recant his profession that Jesus is God, tradition claims he was flayed alive and beheaded for his beliefs. Men do not get skinned alive for what they know is a lie. Nathanael was an eyewitness to the truth of Christ's divinity.

On the night Christ was betrayed, the disciples (eyewitnesses) told Him, "Now we know that *You know all things,* and have no need for anyone to question You; by this we believe that You came from God" (John 16:30). Later, Peter appealed to Christ's omniscience in his own defense: "Lord, You know all things; You know that I love You" (John 21:17).

While most of us like to think we know everything, Jesus demonstrated He actually does. How many fleas are on the back of Napoleon's black cat? Jesus knows. How many stars are in the Andromeda Galaxy? Jesus knows. How many sins have you committed? Jesus knows that too.

5 Jesus Is Omnipotent

Only God is all-powerful. Jesus proved His omnipotence repeatedly by demonstrating authority over nature. Jesus raised people from the dead (Luke 7:11–17; John 11:14–45), produced food for thousands (Matthew 14:15–21; 15:32–38), healed every form of disease (Matthew 4:23; 15:30,31), and ultimately raised Himself from the dead (John 10:17,18).

6 Jesus Claims to Forgive Sin

This was a huge controversy in Jesus' earthly ministry. The Jewish religious leaders were offended when Jesus claimed He could forgive sins. They asked, "Who can forgive sins but God alone?" (Mark 2:7). They understood clearly the implications of His authority, and Jesus did not challenge the truth of their statement that God alone has authority to forgive.

Let me put that scene into perspective. Imagine you are watching the evening news. The anchor reports that a man was walking around town offering to forgive people's sins. You would think this man was delusional at best, insane at worst. Either way, he is most certainly presumptuous. After all, who can forgive sins except the one who was sinned against?

But what if the anchor then showed footage of that man miraculously healing the sick and diseased. You would likely rethink your opinion of that man's sanity and perhaps conclude, "If this man can heal genuine illnesses, maybe he does have the power to forgive sins."

That is precisely what Jesus Christ did. He healed profoundly sick people and announced forgiveness to them. Only God can do even one of those things; Jesus did both. Note this well, Jesus is willing to not only forgive the sick and diseased, He is willing to forgive you. Why would you reject His compassionate offer of forgiveness?

Consider the good news that Jesus is omnipotent, omniscient, and merciful. No matter how sinful you are, your kind, omniscient, and omnipotent God is willing to forgive and cleanse you. You are not beyond hope. You are not out of reach of His powerful benevolent hand. Jesus can save you to the uttermost (Hebrews 7:25).

7 Eyewitnesses Saw Jesus Transfigured

Although Jesus' twelve disciples witnessed His omnipotent miracle working power for three years, they only saw a man; they did not see Jesus in His glorified, divine state. Except for one day.

Jesus took three of His disciples (Peter, James, and John) up a mountain where "He was transfigured before them; and His face shone like the sun, and His garments became as white as light" (Matthew 17:2). Wait, the account gets even more spectacular.

A bright cloud overshadowed them, and behold, a voice out of the cloud said, "This is My beloved Son, with whom I am well-pleased; listen to Him!" *When the disciples heard this*, they fell face down to the ground and were terrified. (Matthew 17:5,6)

That's right, three disciples saw Jesus in His divine state and heard God the Father proclaim that Jesus is God. That is why Peter later wrote, "For we did not follow cleverly devised tales when we made known to you the power and coming of our Lord Jesus Christ, but *we were eyewitnesses of His majesty*. For when He received honor and glory from God the Father, such an utterance as this was made to Him by the Majestic Glory, "This is My beloved Son with whom I am well-pleased"—and *we ourselves heard this utterance made from heaven* when we were with Him on the holy mountain" (2 Peter 1:16–18).

Peter was crucified upside down for these claims. He refused to recant because his eyes and ears didn't lie. You can trust Peter's eye-

witness account and his claim that Jesus is
God.

8 Jesus Receives Worship

Jesus told the devil, "Go, Satan! For it is written, 'You shall worship the Lord your God, and
serve Him only'" (Matthew 4:8). If Jesus Himself were only a creature, He would have been
guilty of rank hypocrisy, for He received worship—frequently.

Before you zoom past this argument, imagine what it looks like for a mere mortal to receive genuine *worship*. We clap for talented
performers, stand when a dignitary enters a
room, and cheer for a stellar performance. But
when was the last time you saw anyone volun-
tarily fall face down and worship another person? Probably never.

Here are a few verses that speak of people
worshiping Jesus, and in every case, He wel-
comed the worship that was offered to Him:

- Matthew 2:11—After coming into the
  house they saw the Child with Mary His

mother; and they fell to the ground and worshiped Him.

- John 9:38—[The man born blind] said, "Lord, I believe." And he worshiped Him.

- Matthew 28:9—And behold, Jesus met [the women coming from His empty tomb] and greeted them. And they came up and took hold of His feet and worshiped Him.

- Matthew 28:16,17— But the eleven disciples proceeded to Galilee, to the mountain which Jesus had designated. When they saw Him [the resurrected Christ], they worshiped Him.

- John 20:28,29—Thomas answered and said to Him, "My Lord and my God!" Jesus said to him, "Because you have seen Me, have you believed? Blessed are they who did not see, and yet believed."

Not once did Jesus rebuke anyone for worshiping Him. In fact, He corrected those who scolded others for worshiping Him, as in Luke 10, when Martha was angry that Mary sat at

His feet. And in Matthew 26, He rebuked the disciples for being indignant when a woman anointed Him with expensive ointment.

Men are applauded. God is worshiped. Jesus was worshiped. Jesus is God.

9 Jesus Raised Himself from the Dead

This is the ultimate miracle of Jesus. Not only did Jesus raise multiple people from the dead, He raised Himself from the dead (Luke 24:5,6). Jesus didn't get dragged to a cross to be executed; He willingly laid down His life and then He raised Himself back to life again (John 10:17,18). This is just one of the reasons Thomas saw the resurrected Christ and exclaimed, "My Lord and my God!" (John 20:27,28).

For two thousand years, skeptics have attempted to disprove the most important claim in Christendom. If Jesus didn't rise from the dead, then they would be right to proclaim the Christian faith is useless and in vain.

Despite every effort by some of the most brilliant minds on the planet, the stubborn, historical fact remains: Jesus Christ actually died, and He actually raised Himself back to life. While people can take their life by suicide, nobody but God can bring Himself back to life. Nobody but Jesus.

Jesus was brutally beaten, scourged with a cat o' nine tails, hung on a cross, and had His side stabbed with a spear. He really was dead. John, a witness to the crucifixion, wrote after describing Jesus' death, that his eyewitness testimony was credible and true, and you can believe in Jesus with confidence (John 19:35).

Additionally, hundreds of people saw the resurrected Christ alive and well as He walked among them, ate with them, and talked with them for forty days. These people had nothing to gain by lying and everything to lose. Hundreds of people were willing to be martyred because they saw Jesus alive after He had most certainly died.

This has huge implications for you. Because Jesus rose from the dead, He promises to raise *you* from the dead. You will be given a body built to last for eternity in heaven...or hell.

Objection!

Proving divinity is infinitely more difficult than proclaiming divinity. Despite the fact that Jesus repeatedly demonstrated He possesses all the attributes of God, some argue, "Jesus never plainly stated, 'I am God.'" Guess what? In a sense, they are correct. And that is perhaps one of the strongest arguments for the deity of Jesus Christ. Here's why.

If you heard a man in Times Square yell, "I am God, believe in me," most likely you would yell back, "You need help, you nutter." And rightly so.

Every time a mere mortal tries to persuade people he is God (far more men make this claim than women, by the way), he says the same predictable thing: "I am God." That is precisely what mere mortals say when they are pretending to be divine.

Jesus never said the words "I am God" because He is not a mere mortal. Jesus makes His claim to deity far more profoundly than a human pretender ever could.

Jesus claimed divine status by identifying Himself with thousands of years of:

- History
- Religion
- Events
- People
- Lineages
- Predictions

In other words, Jesus' claims of deity are credible because He connected Himself to the entire Old Testament, the Jewish religious system, and the history of the nation of Israel.

His claims are valid, profound, unimaginable, and historical.

While it is true that Jesus never said, "I am God," that reality actually strengthens His rightful claim. In other words, Jesus is not a nutter. He is God because His claims are valid, profound, unimaginable, and historical. Prepare to read the irrefutable claims of Jesus Christ.

10 Jesus Ascribes God's Holy Name to Himself

In Exodus 3:14, God told Moses His name is "I AM" (YHWH, pronounced Yahweh or Jehovah). Old Testament Jews believed this name was so holy they refused to speak it for fear of saying it wrong and blaspheming God's holy name.

Instead of saying YHWH (called the tetragrammaton—four letters, appearing almost 6,000 times in the Bible), they used alternative names like Adonai ("my Lord"). Or they would simply call YHWH "the name."

What Jesus says in John 8:58 to an audience of Jewish theologians was so shocking, they picked up stones to kill Him. Why? Because Jesus applied God's name to Himself, saying, "Truly, truly, I say to you, before Abraham was born, I AM."

The religious leaders understood precisely what Jesus was saying. He was telling them He was God, using the name "I AM" for Himself. Jesus could not have made any stronger claim of deity.

If space permitted, we could delve into the series of statements Jesus made about Himself using this name "I AM."

- "I am the way, and the truth, and the life" (John 14:6).

- "I am the good shepherd" (John 10:11,14).

- "I am the door" (John 10:9).

- "I am the bread of life" (John 6:48).

- "I am the Light of the world" (John 9:5).

Each one of those statements was a claim of absolute deity. While skeptics today may not understand what Jesus said, the first century Jewish religious leaders did. That is why they wanted to stone Jesus; He was equating Himself to God.

Not that an exclamation point is needed, but here it is. Jesus said, "I and the Father are one" (John 10:30). Jesus didn't say He and the Father are similar; He confidently claimed to be *one* with God the Father.

Did Jesus claim to be God? Yes, and the way He did proves that He actually is. Jesus also made bodacious claims of divinity by ascribing divine attributes to Himself.

11 Jesus Claimed to Run the Universe

Jesus claims He oversees the operation of divine providence. In Matthew 28:18, Jesus told His disciples, "All authority has been given to Me in heaven and on earth." In John 17:1,2, Christ prayed to the Father, "Glorify Your Son, that the Son may glorify You, even as You gave Him authority over all flesh, that to all whom You have given Him, He may give eternal life…"

Can you see how this claim alone is far more powerful than a predictable, "I am God" declaration? Jesus didn't say, "I am God" the way humans would expect; Jesus said He is divine by His divine assertions.

12 Jesus Claimed Power to Render Final Judgment

In case you have forgotten the high stakes of this study, Jesus' claim to raise *you* from the dead and to judge *you* should get your attention. On the day of God the Father's choosing, God the Son is going to summon you before His judgment seat and render an eternal verdict on you.

Acts 10:42 says Christ was "appointed by God as Judge of the living and the dead" (see also 2 Timothy 4:1). Acts 17:31 says that God "will judge the world in righteousness through a Man whom He has appointed, having furnished proof to all men by raising Him from the dead."

In John 5:22,23, Jesus said, "For not even the Father judges anyone, but He has given all judgment to the Son, so that all will honor the Son even as they honor the Father. He who does not honor the Son does not honor the Father who sent Him." That is a very explicit claim of absolute equality with God the Father.

Notice that Jesus even makes the basis of final judgment the issue of whether someone believes in Him or not. "Truly, truly, I say to you, he who hears My word, and believes Him who sent Me, has eternal life, and does not come into judgment, but has passed out of death into life" (John 5:24).

What verdict will Jesus render on you? What will He say on your day of judgment? Will He thunder, "I never knew you; depart from Me, you who practice lawlessness," or will He smile upon you and proclaim, "Come, you who are blessed of My Father, inherit the kingdom prepared for you from the foundation of the world" (Matthew 7:21–23; 25:31–46)?

It is Jesus who will bring the adopted children of God into the fullness of glorification. Philippians 3:21 says He "will transform the body of our humble state into conformity with the body of His glory, by the exertion of the power that He has even to subject all things to Himself."

13 Jesus Said He Is to Be Believed In

Jesus placed Himself on the highest possible level when He made Himself an object of our faith, saying, "Do not let your heart be troubled; believe in God, believe also in Me" (John 14:1). It would be blasphemy for any mere creature to ask people to put faith in him like they put faith in God.

14 Jesus Said He Is Omnipresent

Jesus Himself claimed to be everywhere all the time (Matthew 18:20). He promised, "I am with you always, even to the end of the age" (Matthew 28:20). Only God can be everywhere at one time.

Scripture says Christ embodies every attribute that is true of Jehovah: "In Him all the fullness of Deity dwells in bodily form" (Colossians 2:9). And Hebrews 1:3 says Christ "is the radiance of His glory and the exact representation of His nature."

Christ embodies every attribute that is true of Jehovah.

Jesus acted and spoke like God because He is God.

15 The Bible Plainly Calls Jesus God

The following Bible verses declare the divinity of Jesus in the strongest of terms. As you read the following verses, exchange the word

"Word" for Jesus Christ because that is who
John is talking about.

> In the beginning was the Word, and
> the Word was with God, and the Word
> was God. He was in the beginning with
> God. All things came into being through
> Him, and apart from Him nothing came
> into being that has come into being.
> (John 1:1–3)

That is a very strong statement about
Christ's deity. Every phrase is significant. "In
the beginning" harks back to Genesis 1:1 and
places Jesus in eternity past, before anything
or anyone was created. B. B. Warfield wrote,

> What is declared is that "in the begin-
> ning"—not "*from* the beginning" but
> "*in* the beginning,"—when first things
> came to be, the Word…already *was*.
> Absolute eternity of being is asserted
> for the Word in as precise and strong
> language as absolute eternity of being
> can be asserted.

The next phrase, "the Word was with God," means that from all eternity, the Word coexisted with God, alongside Him, in personal communion with Him. In Warfield's words, "He has been from all eternity God's Fellow."

But look again at the third phrase in John 1:1, "The Word was God." The linking verb connects the noun on one side with the noun on the other—like an equal sign connects two sides of a mathematical equation. In other words, "The Word = God." To state it plainly, Jesus is God.

There are of course other verses in the New Testament that explicitly call Jesus God.

- Thomas exclaimed, "My Lord and my God!" Jesus did not rebuke him, but commended him for his faith (John 20:28,29).

- Both Titus 2:13 and 2 Peter 1:1 refer to Jesus as "our God and Savior."

- Romans 9:5 says Christ is God over all.

- Philippians 2:6 says Christ existed from all eternity in the form of God.

- 1 John 5:20 says, "We know that the Son of God has come, and has given us understanding so that we may know Him who is true; and we are in Him who is true, in His Son Jesus Christ. This is the true God and eternal life."

One of the clearest verses describing the divinity of Jesus is made by God the Father speaking of His Son: "This is My beloved Son, in whom I am well-pleased" (Matthew 3:17). It is hard to imagine how one could deny such a plain, forceful, and definitive statement.

The case for the deity of Jesus Christ is already insurmountable, but the Bible is not ready to rest its case. The Bible relentlessly presents Jesus as the divine Son of God.

16 Old Testament Titles for God Are Applied to Christ

If you are British, you know the king or queen of England has many titles. Here are just a few:

- Sovereign

- Head of the Commonwealth

- Commander in Chief of the British Armed Forces

- The Lord High Admiral of the Royal Navy

- Supreme Governor of the Church of England

- Defender of the Faith

If a history book filled with reliable eye-witness accounts from the early sixteenth century used any of those titles to describe a man named Henry, what would you conclude? Henry is the King. That is precisely what the Old Testament does. It uses titles for God and applies them to Jesus Christ. Conclusion? Jesus is God.

- In Isaiah 44:6, God is called the first and the last. Revelation 1:17 records Jesus saying, "I am the first and the last."

- In Isaiah 43:11, God calls Himself the only savior. Paul gives Jesus that title in Titus 2:11–14.

- God is described as "the Lord of lords" in
  Deuteronomy 10:17. The last book in the
  Bible gives that title to—you guessed it—
  Jesus Christ (Revelation 17:14).

The Bible identifies Jesus as Jehovah, the
first and the last, Savior, Lord of lords, and
God with us. The Bible gives divine titles to
Jesus because Jesus is divine.

17 Jesus Fulfilled Old Testament Prophecies

God promised to send a Savior for our sin,
and He gave hundreds of prophecies (telling
about His lineage, birth, life, death, and res-
urrection) because He wanted there to be no
mistaking who that Savior would be. Here are
just eight of those prophecies that the Messiah
would fulfill:

The Messiah would be:

- A descendent of Abraham (Genesis 12:3;
  Acts 3:24–26)

- A descendent of David (2 Samuel 7:12–16;
  Matthew 1:1)

- Born of a virgin (Isaiah 7:14; Matthew 1:22,23)

- Born in Bethlehem (Micah 5:2; Matthew 2:1–6)

- Betrayed for thirty pieces of silver (Zechariah 11:12,13; Matthew 26:14,15)

- Brutally beaten (Isaiah 53; Matthew 26:27; 27:26–31)

- Pierced (Zechariah 12:10; John 19:34)

- Resurrected (Psalm 16:8–11; Matthew 28:1–10)

Jesus fulfilled over three hundred prophecies. Case closed.

The odds of one man fulfilling just eight prophecies has been calculated as 1 in 100,000,000,000,000,000. The odds of one man fulfilling forty-eight prophecies is 1 chance in 10^{157} (a statistical impossibility). Jesus fulfilled over three hundred prophecies.

Case closed.

18 The Bible Equates Jesus with God

If any passages in the New Testament quote Old Testament verses using the term "YHWH" and apply those texts to Christ, that would conclusively demonstrate that Jesus is YHWH. Are there any such verses? There certainly are.

- Psalm 23:1 says, "[YHWH] is my shepherd." Jesus very clearly applied that verse to Himself in John 10:11,14 when He said, "I am the good shepherd."

- John the Baptist called Jesus "YHWH" when he used Isaiah 40:3 to describe Jesus: "I am a voice of one crying in the wilderness, 'Make straight the way of the Lord,' as Isaiah the prophet said" (John 1:23).

There are many more clear references in the Old Testament that identify Jesus as Jehovah (e.g., Jeremiah 23:5,6; Acts 2:21; 3:14,15). The inspired Jewish book that was written centuries before the birth of Jesus Christ is relentless and emphatic: the Messiah will be Jehovah.

19 The Bible Ascribes Divine Attributes to Jesus

Not only did Jesus repeatedly claim and demonstrate divinity, the Bible also ascribes attributes to Jesus that only God possesses. In other words, the Bible called Jesus God by telling us that Jesus' nature is exactly like God's.

Jesus is immutable (unchanging)

This attribute could never be true of any created being. God the Father says that God the Son is both immutable and eternal: "You, Lord, in the beginning laid the foundation of the earth, and the heavens are the works of Your hands; they will perish, but You remain; and they all will become old like a garment, and like a mantle You will roll them up; like a garment they will also be changed. But You are the same, and Your years will not come to an end" (Hebrews 1:10–12).

Hebrews 13:8 is another familiar affirmation of the immutability of Christ: "Jesus Christ is the same yesterday and today and forever." The logic is simple; if God alone never changes, and Jesus never changes, then Jesus is God.

Jesus is eternal

The prophet Micah said the Messiah is eternal (Micah 5:2). Jesus claimed He was eternal (John 8:58). Jesus is given titles of eternality. Revelation 22:13 calls Him "the Alpha and the Omega, the first and the last, the beginning and the end."

You and I have a beginning; Jesus does not. Only God is eternal. Jesus is eternal. Jesus is God.

20 Jesus Is Called the Creator and Sustainer of All Things

Jesus Christ is the One who *created* everything that was ever created. "All things came into being through Him, and apart from Him nothing came into being that has come into being" (John 1:3). If that verse is true, Jesus Himself *cannot* be a created being.

Colossians 1:16 says the same thing in more detail, ruling out the possibility that Jesus could be a creature of any kind, including an archangel: "For by Him all things were created, both in the heavens and on earth, visible and invisible, whether thrones or dominions or rulers or authorities—all things have been created through Him and for Him." Verse 17 takes it a step further and pictures Christ not only as Creator but also as the *Sustainer* of all things: "He is before all things, and in Him all things hold together."

The planet you are standing on, the air you are breathing, and the body you inhabit all belong to the Lord Jesus Christ. Everything that exists belongs to Him because He is the Creator of all things.

21 The Earliest Believers Testified to the Deity of Christ

Those who deny the deity of Christ frequently claim that the deity of Christ and Trinitarianism were doctrines imposed on the church in the fourth century by the Nicene Council at the behest of the Roman emperor Constantine. This argument gained popularity from the fictional account Dan Brown wove into *The Da Vinci Code*.

Of course, there is no truth to the claim whatsoever. Biblically minded Christians for two millennia have uniformly affirmed that Jesus Christ is God. Dan Brown may know how to write a compelling book, but Dan Brown clearly doesn't know history.

Around AD 110, Polycarp (a disciple and close associate of the apostle John) wrote an epistle to the church at Philippi. In the benediction to that epistle, he referred to "our Lord and God Jesus Christ and...his Father who raised him from the dead." There's far too much Trinitarian truth in that phrase for anyone who denies the deity of Christ.

Ignatius, another disciple of John's, referred to Jesus as "God in man." He wrote to the church at Ephesus, "Our God, Jesus the Christ, was conceived by Mary according to God's plan, both from the seed of David and of the Holy Spirit."

Justin Martyr, another early church leader just one generation later than Ignatius and Polycarp, wrote that "Christ being Lord, and God the Son of God" was the One who originally appeared to Moses in the burning bush.

Irenaeus, one generation after that, wrote that Christ "was very man, and that He was very God."

Many additional quotes could be cited from the early church fathers, but that should be sufficient to show that Christ's deity was a standard feature of Christian doctrine long before the council of Nicaea in AD 325.

Those who deny the full deity of Jesus Christ are overlooking what the Bible clearly teaches, what Jesus said and did, and what the early church affirmed. They are without excuse.

And that leads us to our final proof for the deity of Jesus Christ. And this one is very personal ... for you.

22 If Jesus Isn't God, We Are Hopeless

What has been highlighted here is by no means an exhaustive study of the evidence of Jesus' deity, but we will look at one more proof that Jesus is God.

Our conscience tells us we have sinned, eternity is written on our heart, and we know

God exists. If we do not have one who can make us right, then we have no hope. As we look at all the offers for hope, there is only One who credibly offers it: Jesus. That is proof that Jesus is God—He is our only credible source of hope.

In John 8:24, Jesus again applies the supreme name of God to Himself: "Unless you believe that I am He, you will die in your sins." A more literal translation would be: "Unless you believe that I AM, you will die in your sins." Here is a more modern way to state what Jesus said, "You will die in your sins if you do not believe that 'I Am Who I Am.'"

While many people like to paint Jesus as a hippie dippy dude who only preached about love, Jesus' words here are downright scary on three levels.

First, Jesus is again claiming divine equality. He clearly equates Himself with God and all that God is. Just as God is holy, Jesus is holy. Just as God is righteous, Jesus is righteous. Just as God is angry with sinners, Jesus is angry with sinners.

Second, Jesus assumes that you and I are sinners. Just like everyone else, we break His laws willingly and repeatedly. We hate, we steal, we lie, we lust; we are racist, sexist, ungrateful, presumptuous, blasphemous; and we certainly don't love our fellow man, let alone God, the way we should. Indeed, we are sinners.

Third, the consequence for sin is damnation. When Jesus said, "You will die in your sins," He didn't mean we would take our last breath while sinning. His words are far more chilling. Jesus was warning us; if we die with our sins unforgiven, we will go to hell eternally.

Whether you currently confess Him as Lord or not, Jesus Christ is the God to whom you will give an account for your life when you die. Jesus will open the books in which He has recorded every sinful deed you have ever committed—or even pondered. Jesus is the One who will render eternal judgment on you.

If you have not repented and trusted in Him, Jesus will pronounce the most horrifying verdict imaginable: "I never knew you; depart from Me, you who practice lawlessness" (Matthew 7:23). No words can describe the horrors that await unforgiven sinners.

In hell there is no hope, no joy, and no relief. The damned will experience only eternal, conscious torment. Jesus Himself will pour out His wrath on condemned sinners forever. Please, let these words frighten you. "It is a terrifying thing to fall into the hands of the living God" (Hebrews 10:31).

While Jesus doesn't take pleasure in sending people to hell (Ezekiel 18:23), He will. But the Bible reveals an additional truth: there is something Jesus much prefers doing.

Jesus loves to save sinners. When Jesus said, "Unless you believe that I am He, you will die in your sins," He was implicitly saying, "But if you do believe in Me, then you won't die in your sins." In other words, if you will repent (turn from your sins) and trust that Jesus is the God-man who died to save you, then you will not go to hell. This is the work that Jesus delights to perform.

Jesus came "to seek and to save that which was lost" (Luke 19:10). The Good Shepherd came to find lost sheep and bring them home.

Jesus came to rescue and restore prodigal sons and daughters. Jesus died to save sinners.

For God so loved the world, that He gave His only begotten Son, that whoever believes in Him shall not perish, but have eternal life. (John 3:16)

Jesus loves to save sinners, and He stands ready to save you, forgive you, help you, and glorify you. Jesus is an offer you should not refuse. You do so at your own peril. More than that, you miss out on being in a right relationship with the most glorious and wonderful Being in the universe.

Jesus Christ split time.
Jesus Christ performs miracles.
Jesus Christ heals the sick.
Jesus Christ has power over nature.
Jesus Christ is omniscient.
Jesus Christ is omnipotent.
Jesus Christ is omnipresent.
Jesus Christ is unchanging.
Jesus Christ is eternal.
Jesus Christ created all things.

Jesus Christ runs the universe.

Jesus Christ is the judge of the entire world.

Jesus Christ is the One we were born to worship.

Jesus Christ is our only hope.

Jesus Christ died for sinners.

Jesus Christ is the only Savior.

Jesus Christ loves to save sinners.

Jesus Christ offers you forgiveness and everlasting life.

Jesus is that amazing. Jesus is that good. Jesus is that...divine. Our response can only be to believe—and to join in the worship of Him at whose name every knee will bow.

Conclusion

The evidence for Jesus' divinity cannot be swept aside or ignored. You either believe it, or you condemn yourself to an unthinkable eternity. Deny the deity of Jesus Christ and you consign your own soul to eternal judgment.

The choice is now yours. You have every reason to repent of your sins and believe in Jesus Christ as your Lord, God, and Savior.

Today, right now, Jesus offers you terms of peace. Take them. Receive Him as your Savior. Join Thomas in saying, "My Lord and my God."

> By this the love of God was manifested in us, that God has sent His only be-gotten Son into the world so that we might live through Him.
> In this is love, not that we loved God, but that He loved us and sent His Son to be the propitiation for our sins. (1 John 4:9,10)

No doubt you have seen or heard objections to the claim that Jesus is the divine Son of God. We encourage you to read thoughtful responses to most of those critiques here:

gotquestions.org